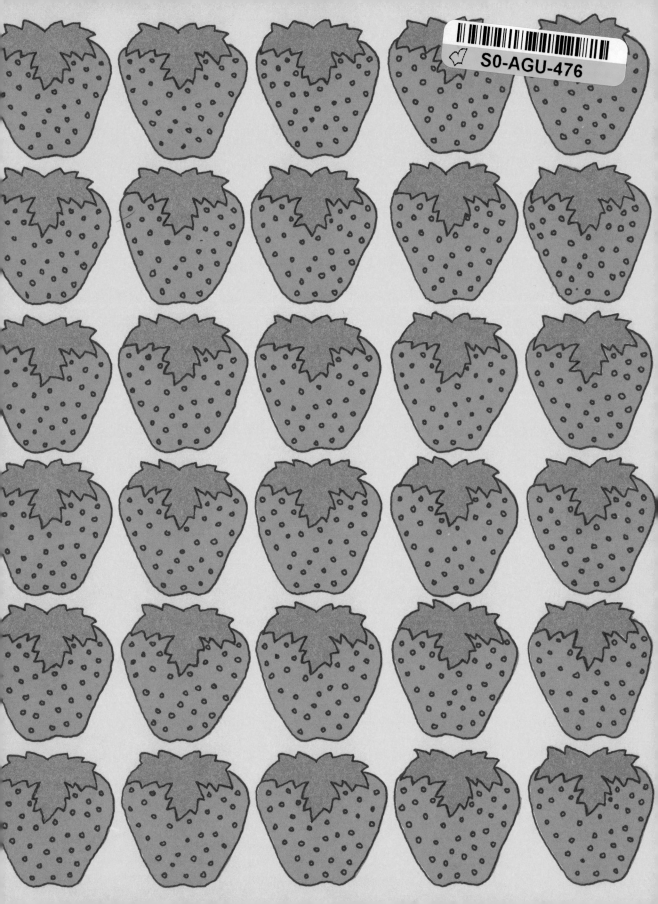

this
strawberry library
of first learning
book
belongs to

*this book
is for
Pauline,
the grandmother*

Weekly Reader Books Edition

an animal alphabet

by Richard Hefter

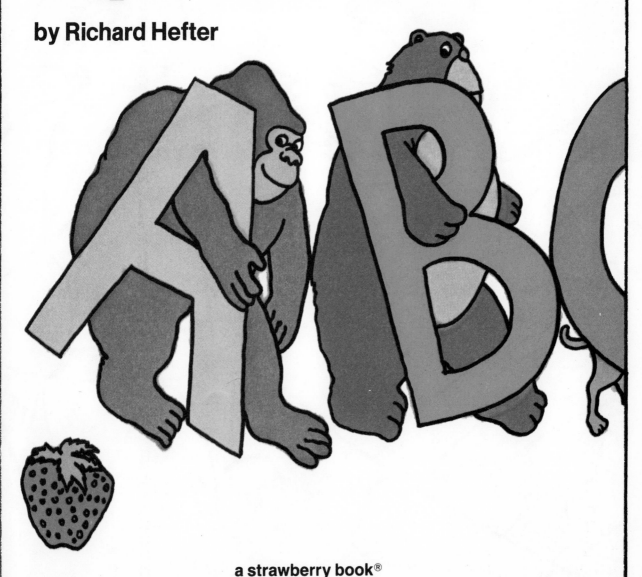

a strawberry book®

A DIGNIFIED DONKEY
IS DRIVING A DUMP TRUCK.

ENGINEER ELEPHANTS
EAT EASTER EGGS.

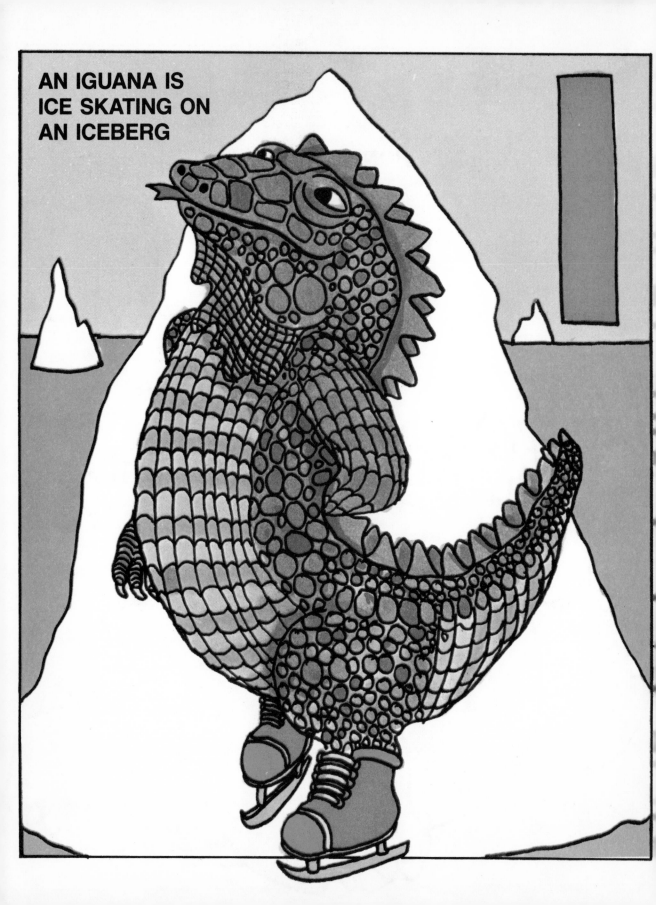

A KANGAROO'S KIOSK IS FIT FOR A KING.

A NERVOUS
AND NAUTICAL
NARWHALE IS
NICE.

A RABBIT WHOSE ROWBOAT HAS JUST RUN THE RAPIDS IS VERY RELIEVED AND REALLY SHOULD REST.

A UNICORN UNICYCLIST
UNDER AN UMBRELLA

U

A ZANY ZEBRA ZIPS
BY IN A ZEPPELIN.

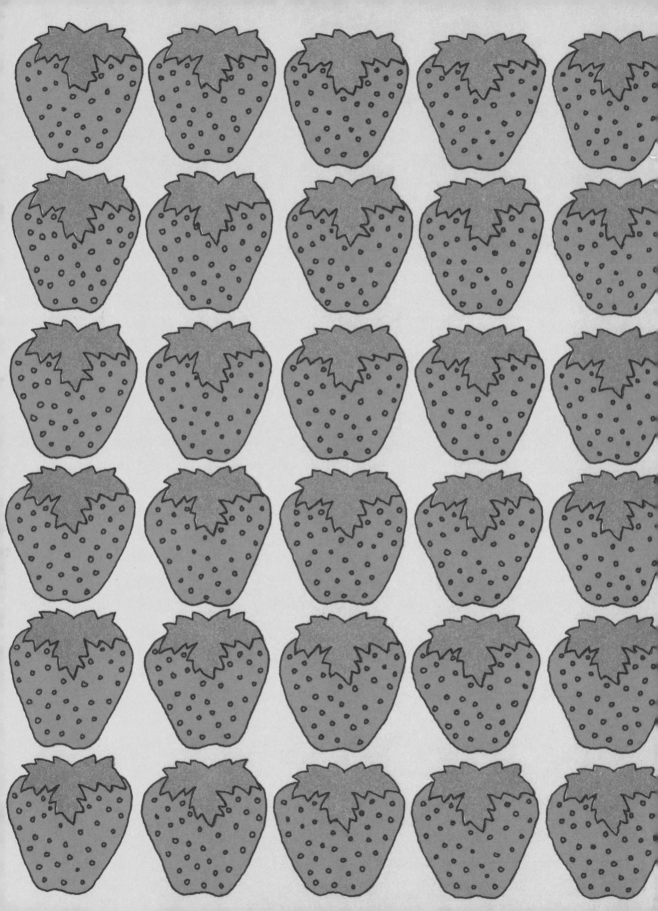